Print Wacky Sentences

First and Second Grade Writing Practice Workbook (Reproducible)

by Julie Harper

Print Wacky Sentences: First and Second Grade Writing Practice Workbook (Reproducible)

Children's Books > Education & Reference > Words & Language

Children's Books > Education & Reference > Education > Workbooks

ISBN 10: 1475076673

EAN 13: 978-1475076677

Table of Contents

Introduction

The goal of this unique writing workbook is to engage children and motivate learning through the use of creativity. Children enjoy reading wacky sentences like, "My teacher kissed a lizard." Exercises like these help to make learning fun, whether in the classroom or at home.

This *Print Wacky Sentences* writing workbook focuses on writing complete sentences. Students who need more practice writing individual letters or single words may benefit from using this workbook in combination with a basic writing workbook which focuses on practicing letters and short words.

Three sections of this workbook help students develop their writing skills at a variety of levels:

- ✓ In Part 1, students practice handwriting motions by tracing dotted sentences like, "Two rabbits slept on a fox's head."
- ✓ Part 2 advances to help students begin to write on their own. In this section, students first trace a dotted sentence and then copy the sentence onto a new line. The three traditional horizontal lines are included as a guide – solid top and bottom lines plus a dashed middle line help students master the relative heights of the letters, and to write across the page in straight lines.
- ✓ Part 3 gives solid sentences like, "Six elephants jumped over a giraffe," instead of dotted sentences. At this stage, students practice their handwriting without first tracing the letters.

May your students or children improve their writing skills and enjoy reading and writing these wacky sentences.

Uppercase Alphabet

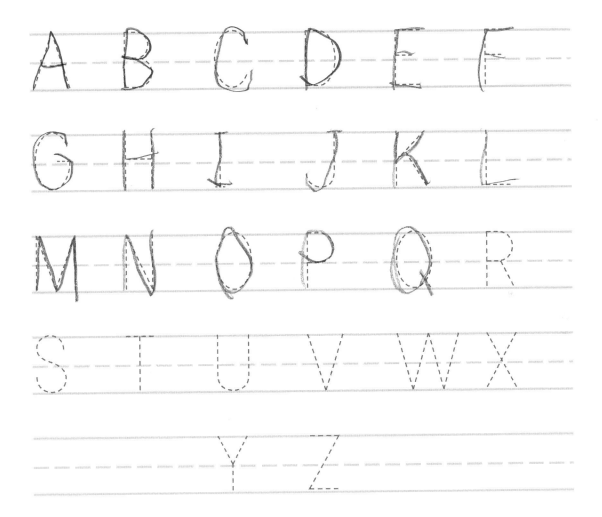

Lowercase Alphabet

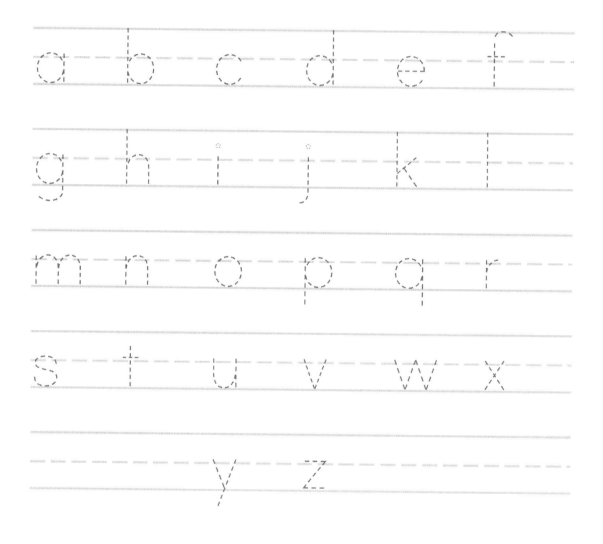

Part 1 Trace Wacky Sentences

Part 1 Instructions: Trace directly over these dotted sentences.

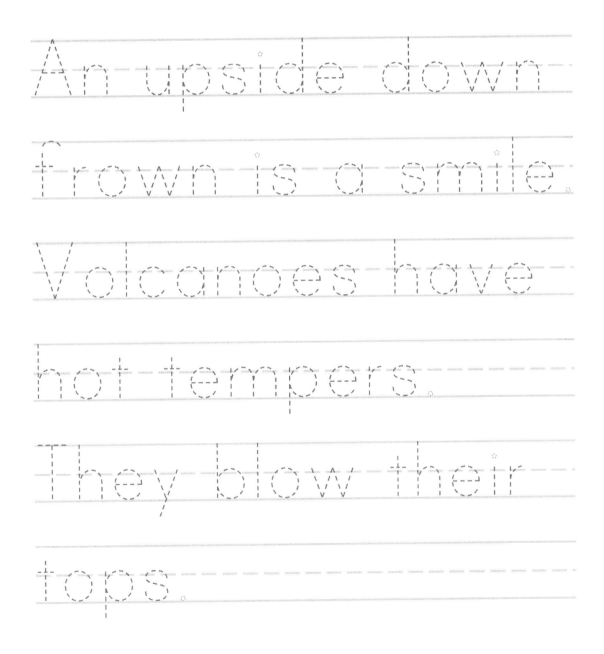

An upside down

frown is a smile.

Volcanoes have

hot tempers.

They blow their

tops.

Our little brother

howls at the full

moon.

Elephants carry

their own

showers.

Homework is fun

when it is done.

My shadow went

on vacation

today.

Wiggle worms

squiggle while

they giggle.

Six crows ate my

corn for lunch.

A spaceship
took six mice to
the moon for a
cheese snack.
Do roadrunners
walk when they
are tired of
running?

Cheetahs ran a

race against

five snails, and

lost.

Black cats and

ladders love

Friday the

thirteenth.

After Christmas,

a clown

borrowed

Rudolph's red

nose.

A policeman

tagged me and

said I was it.

Our class took

our pets to the

petting zoo.

Wily roadrunners

chase fast

coyotes when

they are bored

and mischievous.

When I scream

for ice cream,

the ice cream

screams back.

A dog sleeps in

a tree while a

cat sleeps in his

doghouse.

We kicked
soccer balls at
the bowling
alley on Friday.
A monkey got
detention for
pretending to be
a student.

Five monkeys
got speeding
tickets for going
too fast.
Last Halloween,
I did tricks and
gave treats to
Goblins.

Have you ever
seen a cat chase
a computer
mouse?
The wolf turned
into a man
during the full
moon.

One time a

green lime ate

thyme and

turned to slime.

The moon smiled

at me and it was

two in the

afternoon.

A thousand
snakes slithered
over the
skyscraper.
There are
rainbows. Why
aren't there
snowbows?

Rugs are lazy
because they
are always lying
around.
An artist drew a
pencil with an
eraser. Imagine
that!

Your principal
likes to make
mud angels on
rainy days!
We balanced
eggs on our
noses when we
danced.

Can a potato

with fifty eyes

see in all

directions?

My little brother

repeats

everything our

parrot says.

If you see an
alligator smile,
you are way too
closet
Koala bears
change the light
bulbs at the
ballpark.

Wolves howl at
the sun on
Mondays and
Fridays.
Venus shook
hands with
Jupiter during
the eclipse.

The billy goat
was so silly
when he ate the
wacky words.
I caught my
grandparents
playing with my
dolls.

The whale
emptied our pool
when he did a
cannonball.
Have you ever
seen a hippo
ride a merry-go-
round?

Lollipops kissed

her nose and

tickled her

armpits.

Lazy birds

bought sweaters

instead of flying

south.

Two mice

chased a cat

who tried to

steal their

cheese.

If a fly eats

butter, will he be

a butterfly?

Three pink

elephants pulled

our school bus

to the zoo.

Jugglers juggle

purple potatoes

and juicy

tomatoes!

The glue stuck

the stapler, and

the paper cut

the scissors.

A fire hydrant

chased a dog

and almost

caught him.

The cow milked
the farmer first
thing in the
morning.
I put my pillow
under my feet
so they could
sleep.

A blimp is a

plane that ate

too much

Thanksgiving

dinner.

Penguins played

dodgeball with

polar bears.

I walk a mile

along the Nile

while I smile all

the while.

Ducks love

spaghetti with

wormballs and

sauce.

We had a
screaming party
at the library
last month.
Carrots were
playing golf with
grapes on the
counter.

His car has

square tires and

walks like a

lizard.

I found an

elephant sitting

at our dining

room table.

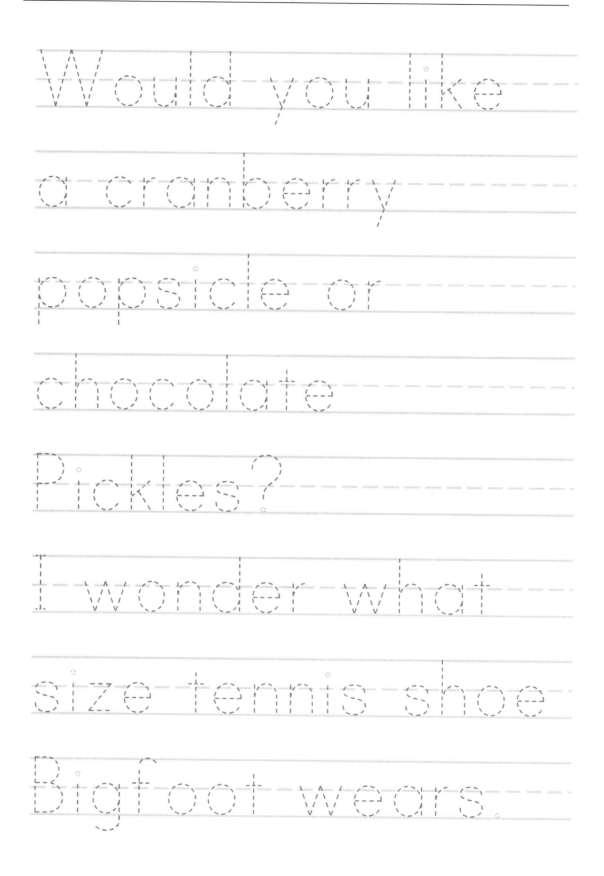

Would you like
a cranberry
popsicle or
chocolate
Pickles?

I wonder what
size tennis shoe
Bigfoot wears.

Our bus driver

picked us up in

a tractor

yesterday.

Rainbows must

be sad because

they always

frown.

A pink mink likes
to wink at the
mirror above the
sink.
Santa Claus
brought me
Easter eggs on
Halloween.

My dog loves to

Wear jeans on

Sunday evening.

My neighbor

threw a party

for the neon

green lion and

friends.

A damsel in
shining armor
saved a knight
in distress.
Her doctor gave
himself a shot
to make her feel
better.

On Thanksgiving,
turkeys give
thanks when we
eat ham.
It only rained
under my
umbrella when I
closed it.

If we eat our
cake, we get
chicken for
dessert.
A silly bear
shaved his fur
and sold it for
honey.

Be nice to ghosts. They might be afraid of people. I wore pajamas to school and went to sleep in a suit.

Fish held nets
above the water
to catch birds.
Two purple bear
cubs sled down
the mountain
on a yellow and
red toboggan.

Sour grapes like
to eat sweet
candy and
gummy balls.
Scuba divers
sound funny if
they use helium
tanks.

The giraffe
crawled under
the elephant to
get his baseball.
I ate chocolate
covered carrots
for breakfast
this morning.

We wear our
clothes inside
out so they don't
get dirty.
Pigs and cows
laughed. I
guess it was the
funny farm.

The sun stopped
and changed
direction. Was
it lost?
Three cheetahs
were ticketed
for going too
slow.

Part 2 Trace and Copy Wacky Sentences

Part 2 Instructions: Trace directly over these dotted sentences and then rewrite them on the blank lines below.

Chickens eat
vegetable beef
soup when they
are sick.

There is a raccoon living in my locker at school.

Banjos were
played by three
rats nibbling
cheese.

Cold cocoa is served with hot ice cream on warm days.

Tiny green men
with funny ears
visited our
school.

Seven garden snails rode on the back of a giant tortoise.

The skunk wears
toilet water
perfume and
before shave.

We like to play
tennis with
skates and
hockey sticks.

The big bad
piggy blew the
little wolf's
house down.

Four furry birds

ran after a cat

that had purple

feathers.

It rained peanut
butter and jelly
sandwiches last
night.

The vacuum cleaned the driveway for my mother.

The mailman

puts postage

stamps on his

cheeks.

The gorilla tried
to fix the car
using a monkey
wrench.

Nine elephants
play baseball
while our team
eats peanuts.

Tuna fish and
Cheerios are
yummy for my
tummy.

She brought a
pet snake to
school to play
jump rope.

My dog cooked

dinner and my

cat washed the

dishes.

Pizza flavored
gum is better
than broccoli
flavored cake.

A galaxy tapped me on my shoulder to ask for the time.

A cat barked
and a dog
meowed, so we
mooed.

Dad parks his
truck in the
family room on
Fridays.

Zookeepers are locked up in cages every other Tuesday.

I can run back-
wards while
juggling six ripe
tomatoes.

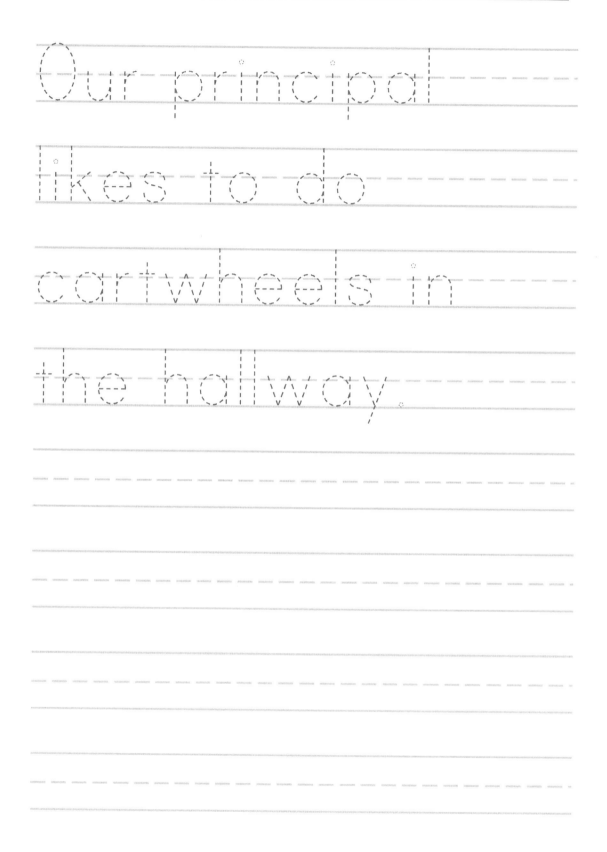

Our principal
likes to do
cartwheels in
the hallway.

An alien came to my house to ask how to get to Mars.

The tooth fairy
came down the
chimney on
Halloween.

I love to eat

chocolate fries

with catsup on

them.

The spaghetti
tasted like
gummy bears.
Delicious!

Six elephants jumped over a giraffe using a trampoline.

The horse rode
the cowboy all
the way across
the town.

My teacher brought a skunk to school in her backpack.

Jumping beans
are how our dog
got stuck on the
roof.

Grandpa brought
a goat in my
closet to eat the
mess.

He sneezed
through his ear
and coughed out
his nose.

My reflection
likes to dance
while I brush my
teeth.

Most of the
teachers wore
diapers on
casual Friday.

Snowflakes floated up to the clouds last Christmas.

Zoo animals took
a field trip to
our school last
week.

I ate my dog's
homework to see
how much he
liked it.

Part 3 Copy Wacky Sentences Without Tracing

Part 3 Instructions: Rewrite these sentences on the blank lines below without tracing.

Two rabbits slept on a fox's head.

Our teacher
kissed a lizard
and it kissed
her back.

When I bit a
vampire, he
turned into a
human being.

My toilet burps
when it flushes,
then says,
'Excuse me.'

Skunks love perfume and long-stemmed red roses.

All the kids wore beards and mustaches to class.

I thought today was the day before tomorrow. Oh, it is!

The computer mouse ran off with my cheese sandwich.

Have you ever seen a tooth-less cow chew bubblegum?

Checkers is hard
when there are
three colors of
squares.

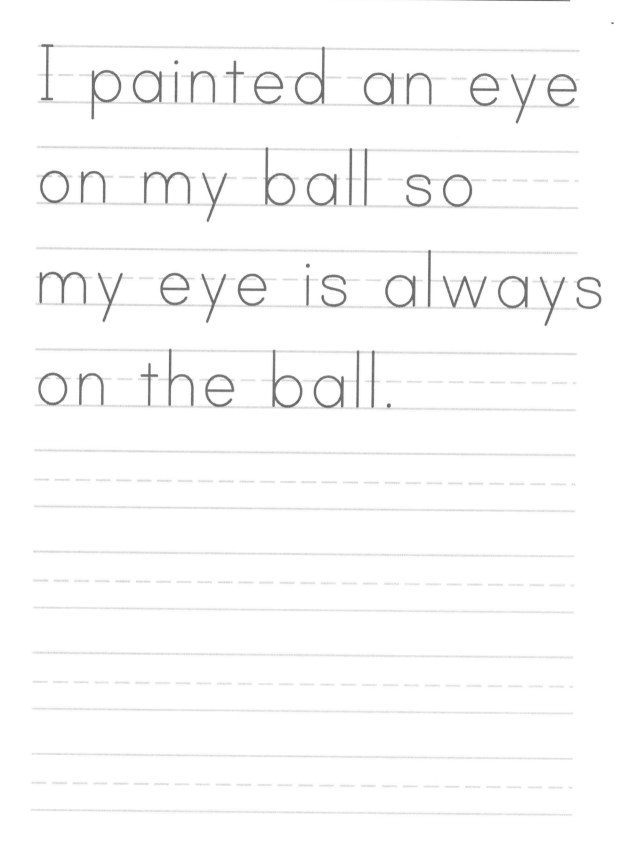

I painted an eye
on my ball so
my eye is always
on the ball.

We got to dance on our desks during class yesterday.

Santa gave me cookies and milk, and I gave him toys.

The airplane
tiptoed across
the sky to save
fuel.

A hungry banana
peeled an
orangutan during
recess.

Lions roared
when they saw
the moon jump
over the cow.

There is a seal
living in our pool
who likes to
play ball.

The only doors
at my house are
on floors and
ceilings.

Mechanics wearing monkey suits swing from the axles.

The principal expelled the camel for spitting in class.

My piggy bank
ate my money
and won't give
back.

A chicken was born on the day my brother was hatched.

Students balanced fruit on their heads during assembly.

We ate caramel covered hot dogs and peas for lunch.

Some penguins were riding camels down the highway.

My dad likes peanut butter and jellyfish sandwiches.

I met a yellow polka-dotted ladybug on Wednesday.

A big jack-o-
lantern scared
the black cat
on Halloween.

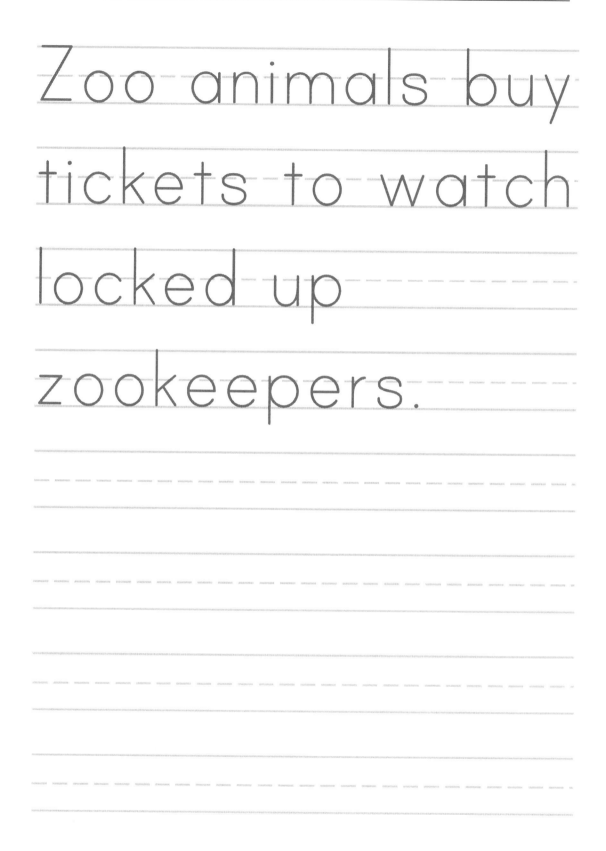

Zoo animals buy tickets to watch locked up zookeepers.

Dancing on the moon three days in a row is hard work.

I rode a
dinosaur to
school, and he
licked the nurse.

Oh no! I forgot what I am suppose to remember.

Alligators play baseball in the snow every Monday.

Captain America eats hero sandwiches and drinks 'superade.'

Pancake syrup
on cheese pizza
is delicious for
breakfast.

I wish we could
declare
chocolate to be
a vegetable.

Frogs laugh and sing while the fish blow bubbles.

At the beach, I
dog paddle
while my dog
swims.

My sweet dreams scared off the nightmares.

Maybe so, maybe not, I really don't know. Do you?

Workbooks by Julie Harper

✓ *Letters, Words, and Silly Phrases Handwriting Workbook (Reproducible): Practice Writing in Cursive (Second and Third Grade).*

✓ *Wacky Sentences Handwriting Workbook (Reproducible): Practice Writing in Cursive (Third and Fourth Grade).*

✓ Print Uppercase and Lowercase Letters, Words, and Silly Phrases: Kindergarten and First Grade Writing Practice Workbook (Reproducible).

✓ Print Wacky Sentences: First and Second Grade Writing Practice Workbook (Reproducible).

Made in the USA
San Bernardino, CA
03 March 2014